We Are All Just Animals & Plants

Published by Metatron
www.onmetatron.com
305-5555 Ave. de Gaspé, Montreal QC H2T 2A3

Copyright © Alex Manley, 2016
All rights reserved
ISBN 978-1-988355-01-6

Editing | Guillaume Morissette
Layout and book design | Ashley Opheim
Cover art | Charlotte Picotte

First edition
First printing

We acknowledge the support of the Canada Council for the Arts, which last year invested $153 million to bring the arts to Canadians throughout the country.

For Shuang, who helped me grow.

Contents

Habitat   1

I: Animals

Mars & The Black Hole   5
Naming Rights   7
Bird Brain   9
Camera   11
All I Want   13
Butterfly Knife   18
The Natural Sciences   20

II: Assorted Paraphernalia

Prometheus II   25
Black Squirrel   27
Bad Reputation   29
Winter Solstice   31
Scotch Bonnet   33

III: Plants

Bonnie & Clyde Nite   37
Strange Powers   39
Pamela Isley   41
Belabor   43
The Lip Of   44
Garden Variety   53
The Left-Hand Path   55

Noahtic   57

Habitat

I'm atom.
Up and sprouting.

Coming, seeing, divvying heights.
A foetus in the gauze of antique pages.

Calligraphy pens split open in the middle
like Darwin's finches, Linnaean

nomenclature's sheen. Time-lapse clips
of flowering cacti drip from the canopy.

Catch from the caruncula my crocodile
tears. Mark the cells on the door frame.

Punnett's squares wrinkle in the heat, wither.
Burst. I'm Mendel. I'm phenotypes. Study

my modifications. Farm me. Till
me. Monetize my instinct. Cash my crop.

Watch me dance, like a bee. Watch
the patterns. Do the math. All the

fundamental things comply. You've got to
know that you're bringing out

all the viral in me. Life's pandemic
contagion. A fauve machine.

I'm licking my chops, mechanically
animal. I'm hatching claws. Nature,

red of tooth and syringes. I'm sprouting
leaves, vines, tendrils

of smoke, forest fires. I'm ash.
I'm dust. I'm sprouting.

A

I: ANIMALS

Mars & The Black Hole

i
When we wake up, it's already one
and the light sits there in your room like a shy friend,

unobtrusive, too polite to rouse us from our sleeping in.
The walls are deer skull, bone-white and I am naked.

ii
When you leave to get us breakfast in bed, I check the internet
on my phone. We eat last night's remaining bagels

with cream cheese and feed each other pieces of mango
the way you feed me poems from your pink Neruda chapbook,

first in Spanish, then in English,
fingers to lips, wet and sticky.

iii
When we fuck, we borrow your roommate's last condom,
and when we shower we wash each other, each a child by turn.

iv
When we step out, you take me ten minutes out of the way
to show me a quiet spot you like, a little bridge,

a piece of road over lines and lines of train tracks.
It's endearing in its unimpressiveness, that you would

care to share something so small with me.
The train tracks stretch out before us, below us, for us,

distance beckoning. I've kissed girls on bridges before,
but never when it was this cold out.

Naming Rights

There are names for trees, actually—
black ash, pin cherry, slippery elm.

The trick is not to know them
when you're walking through the forest.

There are names for all sorts of things,
So why shouldn't there be names for

the gradient before the camera focuses,
the way it's always pink or grey;

for all the futures we invent, which will
one day be pasts that never happened;

for the conversations I imagine we will have
the next time we meet, the way you take stage direction;

for the pictures you show everyone, that make me ache
like a hungry little turtle whose jaws are always snapping.

Why shouldn't there be a name for the kiss I give you
when I catch myself trying to pretend I've fallen in love—

the way you say you have on your secret blog—
like black ash, pin cherry, slippery elm?

Bird Brain

Open up the ribcage. Let the wings beat like drums.
Potential and fragility are two sides of the same

skinny bill, twisted and folded into a crane. I am
six years old, and a smiling rich blonde girl is coming

over for a playdate. We are building a pillow fort on
the wrong side of the tracks. Her mother drove

her over in a Mercedes-Benz. What lessons do
we learn at that age? Is that the reason I've always

been a sockeye hopping upstream, a hawk battling
the gulf wind? Is this human nature or just cards

and coincidences? Can you understand why I'm
starting to feel hunted, why I'm now trapped in a

glass case of devotion, a '50s phone booth beset
by the diving falcons, by the wheeling gulls? I

had first read it in a library book at school; now
still can't shake that fear that someday, something

will turn and they'll all come for us. At that point,
there is no why—although in college, I watched

a fat, sniffling bearded man tell me it was about
a mother's anxiety. But when I finally met yours

she was friendly, sat down on the bed and touched
my leg, although she probably didn't mean it in

that way. Later, out walking, a dead cat lying in
the alley made you scream. The suddenness of it.

Camera

I am a dolly rig
in this greenhouse, I

roll through the rooms
on rails, brushing against

the leaves. It is dark. Quiet.
The place doesn't close until

nine and we are taking advantage.
We are alone. You want to fuck here,

but I don't. You say you don't think that
people are taking good care of the plants.

We sit down at the wrought-iron table and
make hearts with our hands. It has been half

a year since we first kissed. Passing some purple
flowers, you wonder aloud whether they might be

carnivorous. On our way out I see something—a raccoon, a little shadow scurrying from the room,

then it's gone.

All I Want

Do you remember the scenes from the dreams
I told you about? The way I was a deer,

and you were the moon, the candy peaches, the
mango strips? The way the light was—

not angry or loving, but just there? Because all I
want to do is keep playing this game a little

bit longer, to stay with you in this Schrödinger's
Cat relationship until the summer,

when we can fall apart from each other and
each into something new,

like two snakes untangling, or a gilt statue
splitting down the middle,

and each half sinking to the glittering bottom
of a different swimming pool.

All I want to do is write about the things in
the ocean, the plant and animal life,

the dust motes slowly making their way
through sunbeams, glinting,

skin cells from all the people who were born
on land and died in the water.

No one ever tells you not to date the ocean.
The things you get yourself into

and then can't get yourself back out of again.
All I want is for it to be springtime

at the end of this endless winter and for this snow
to be dirty little trickles by the curb,

so I can be a new me, and buy short-sleeved
floral button-ups, and wear sunglasses,

and make new bad choices with the whiskey
bottles lined up on the bookcase.

All I want to do is come into work a little bit
later every day, my beard a little longer,

and spend twelve to fifteen dollars on lunch,
Facebook stalk my old therapist

in the jungle of my browser tabs, and think
disinterestedly about my mental health,

and wonder if people can tell that I'm Febrezing
my clothes instead of washing them.

Because all I want is a time machine and to figure
out which moment I want to return to—

back to the cavernous empty classroom, so
you can rebuff me again,

back to the roller-derby first date, so you can
kiss me again, back to your tiny room,

so you can make me cry again, with that quiet little
song you played like a slap in the face.

All I want is to sit somewhere on the real grass
in the real sunlight, as simple as

a line from a poem in a font with no serifs, and
use my phone to check your Twitter,

like I'm running my finger along the edge of a
stolen hunting knife, the one we used

to pop the top off that Jarritos Lime we mixed
with vodka the last time you came over,

and let your rushing emotions wash over and drain
from my body, revealing my weak spots—

the little things I remember, the ghosts of the bruises
you left at the doorstep of my clavicle,

the fact that my hair is giving up and retreating,
the way I trot through people's lives,

like a horse with blinders on. A horse that was
blind the whole time.

All I want to do is ask you some questions, like: Is that
an occult hand I see guiding all of this?

Are four hundred texts too many to send in a single Groundhog
Day and night of misfortune?

Which one of us will be left holding the bag the cat
got out of, who else will suck the snot

from your glowering face when you're lying on a midnight
sidewalk, will you draw me close,

like a stick and poke? Because all I want to do is
make a home for myself in the sad crags

of your brain, like a flightless bird making a nest,
or a small child holding an Etch-a-Sketch,

something that will last long enough to let me
watch you ebb, like the tide,

and find some other rough cliffs to crush yourself
against, just like you tweeted.

Butterfly Knife

In Audubon's *Birds of America*,
we discover the King Eider.

In Grimes' room, while Grimes is on the road,
the cat is named after Vladimir Lenin.

In the movie shoot version of the relationship,
my exes mime conversation at dinner tables behind us.

In the "Sorry" video, you slip through
the dancing colours, uncaught. In time,

I make you cry. Paper tiger. In anger,
you tattoo your face in pen, call yourself a witch.

In the alleyway, after dark, we do it in silence.
I wait for strangers to intervene, but none do.

You ask me to hit you. You make me cry. In time,
your desire swallows everything, consequences especially.

I always see you in Rihanna's face, and I see
a dark flower in an unlit greenhouse in yours. If there

wasn't more to life than your basement bedroom, we could have
grown old together, like that smiling woman and her cat, in Japan.

In time, we could have been one of those couples
other couples are afraid of.

The Natural Sciences

Instead of writing a poem about this mess I made,
what if I wrote a poem about the natural sciences?

Gravity, biology, phrenology,
black holes, spectrums of light,

how the placebo effect is weakening. Octopi
are just like humans, for instance—they can

bend, fold, warp
their frames, reach to touch

each body part with other body parts. I think
about this a lot, the trap of animal bodies—

ungulates, fish, fowl,
most insects, non-snake reptiles—

how married to (and divorced from) their bodies
they must be, how held down. They can't

inspect, touch, rub,
scratch itches, palpate at will;

need to rope the outside world
into collaborating—

partners, strangers, tools,
weather patterns, acts of God—

but we are a class apart,
a different breed, like

arthropods, invertebrates, ouroboros,
twisting octopi, grabbing and crawling

and scrabbling their way through inkwell lives.
I hope you find yourself in Australia.

II: ASSORTED PARAPHERNALIA

Prometheus II

i
It is a sci-fi movie prequel. But the tech is superior. Is that a
time paradox, or do you believe in the theory of devolution.

ii
There is a hum for you growing in my gut, like a xenomorph,
while the garlic in the belly of my fridge is sprouting

bright green explosions, unearthly little child-things I
crush flat beneath a knife. Would you stop running

into me, pretending you want to talk to me at parties,
it's not healthy, I am losing my head all over again,

in a mutual friend's backyard, it's dark and I am floating,
that's worth drinking to, I'd imagine.

iii
I am watching the many films of us backwards and forwards;
some of the moments seem non-canonical. I am releasing a

new cut with a crucial missing scene: The projector
shows a flipped-over tortoise, struggling, in the desert.

iv
You are with me at the South Pole,
you are with me in the escape pod.

You are moving your body to the songs I say I like,
you are keeping me alive, for your own selfish purposes.

You are beautiful, like a white cobra, can I pet you,
big things have small beginnings.

Black Squirrel

Sitting on the newly lint-rolled couch,
I watch the cat breathe in

the sun. I hear you got a job tending
bar somewhere nearby.

It's been two years now since we
last saw each other,

although I've been in town a lot
more lately. I guess

you're like the ink that bled out
of my pen when I

took it out of my pocket on the plane
in. It got everywhere and

the stains stayed on my skin, ringed
my fingers, tips and

nails. It'll fade eventually. Yesterday
I saw a black squirrel

behind a fence in a park. I'd forgotten
they even existed.

Bad Reputation

No snares in the drums. So alone in so much of me.
I'm not in love with you, or anyone. I'm in love with

tension. Do you know how this thing is played? You're
living in the past. I've entered the second phase of

construction on your broken heart. Can you see the
difference? Day by day it gets worse. All this talk of

phases. My brain is a body going through heat failure.
Thoughts shorting out like organs shutting down, until

all that's left is a corner backing in on itself. No, no, no,
not me. I think about her because she looks like you,

that's transference, and she helps me forget about you,
and in a few weeks someone else will help me forget about

her. My brain is a daisy chain. My brain is a broken piece
of machinery that was once meant to strike something

now flailing rhythmically through the air, never in danger
of contact. My brain is a heart with ADHD, a knife in a

toaster, a toaster in the bath. My brain is the word "mouth
feel" in pink all caps Gotham bold superimposed on a giant

picture of a tongue. My brain is a Tinder match with a girl
I met in a bar last year, who likes my Instagram pictures

sometimes, who looks just like you, only her hair is curlier.
Can you see? So why should I care about a bad reputation?

Just phase it out. Somehow you stole that song from me,
just because we watched it once together on YouTube on

your couch. This is how I keep time, watching the hours
since you were last on Facebook grow. It never gets better.

Winter Solstice

The afterburners kick out in the nice
farmer's market that everybody loves.

"Don't you ever get tired of being so
aware?" It's cold outside, and the fridges

are all full of little bodies. There's cotton
in the flower stalls and a man playing

an acoustic guitar. I buy two bottles of
sugar cane cola. It snows Instagram flakes.

We talk about a lot of things: Kanye,
Detroit, Louis Farrakhan, feminism.

Look at all the tall buildings. My friends
are just as sure of themselves as me.

We stack arguments like wooden blocks,
and watch them teeter. Outside, the

snow is trapping the city like an animal
in a tarp. It's dark. Walking home,

I wonder if that little ghost of mine will
end up at the secret bar we're all going

to later. The other versions of her are in
Paris, Toronto, Starbucked in morning

metro cars, wedged into booths in nice
restaurants I'll never go to again, riding

off in slow taxis with other, taller, even
more nonchalant intellectuals than me.

Scotch Bonnet

i
Some people are photographers,
dancers, chemists, lepidopterists,

professors, architects, diplomats.
There are even people who are surgeons.

ii
Somehow they find use for their perversities, but me,
I just have all these bonsai trees growing in my torso.

It's pathetic, I imagine them whispering, a grown man
who can't stop accumulating miniatures. I study

the way the roots snake; the way the leaves grow,
the way the flowers blossom, wither and fall.

iii
Some days I can't tell if I'm the panther
or the mom-jeaned zoo-goer, cotton candy in hand. Nature

is tricky like that. When I bought those scotch bonnets—
little colour clusters crowded under the cellophane—

and made to cut one up, something came out
of that pale green lump. Left me coughing

for hours afterward. A tickle in my mouth.
A ghost in my throat.

iv
Sometimes what you bring home is more
than what you bargained for.

P

III: PLANTS

Bonnie & Clyde Nite

i
When the movie is over, the two beautiful stars are dead.
As you unlock your bike, we decide to go to a tiki bar nearby.
Like us, it's only a few weeks old, and full of promise.

We walk slow and try to fill the air with words.
At the bar we order the drink that comes in a coconut.
There are little red things in it.

We take turns sipping from our coconut. I don't
want you to put your face close to mine if you don't want to.
But I want you to *want* to put your face close to mine.

Are they little strawberries or little flowers, you say.
A fruit is just an explosion of a flower, frozen in time, I say.
That's beautiful, you say. Maybe I'll put it in a poem, I say.

ii
When the coconut is empty we eat little bits of it. The waiter
comes by. We talk about jobs. Apartments. Fathers. Trips.
Politics. You have work early tomorrow morning.

iii
When we go to leave we meet the bar's owner. He's a lot like me—another lonely man who doesn't want us to go just yet. He keeps talking to us. We all do shots of a grassy liqueur.

We both shake his hand. We've touched him more than we've touched each other. We walk north. It's so cold. I have to pee. You've got your bike. It's not *raining*-raining. But it is raining.

iv
When I get to work the next morning I listen to "Wuthering Heights" with just one earphone. I think of Warren Beatty's sunglasses. How that missing lens foreshadowed his death.

The date was a trick question that I answered too straight.
The date was a hedge maze that I came out of too quickly.
I talk to my friend from a few cubicles over on Gchat.

you know those days where you kinda
put on a bad mood like a suit of armor
Maybe I'll put that in a poem, I think.

Strange Powers

We are all in our own little
cults. Sun. Moon. Heaven's
gates. We all meet strangers

with something to sell: baubles,
trinkets, ways of life, carrying
around briefcases, or wrapped

in white robes, trying to wriggle
these people into our grasp,
little games of thumb war.

This thing is like a video
I saw on YouTube once,
a praying mantis stumbling,

smashed over and over
by a merciful human hand.
Watch as a long, thin string

of blackness winds its way
out of the crushed abdomen,
dancing an occult dance

to a tune only it can hear.
We are all puppets to our
own personal Gepettoes.

We are all in our own little
life cycles. The Kool-Aid
wants so badly to be drunk.

Pamela Isley

Watch a new person grow over top of you, like
ivy. Watch insects replace the megafauna.
Protein is protein is protein, even

when it keeps on shrinking. We
still crave the disgusting little morsels.
We make sparks like a sweating Ivy Leaguer

trying to hotwire an all-black Hemi 'Cuda. It
was in a picture book. Hidden under
the pillow on my parents' bed.

Flip for a bit and discover the
vines swirling about, a jungle aura,
something in the air that could make lips

prick, make something stir in little boys. I guess
you had been on my mind for years, or just
that feeling of losing your compass,

*la mise en abyme, quand tout bascule
dans le vide*, and the power of a single kiss
to unstitch figure from ground, signal from noise,

black from white until it's all television snow and
the intravenous tendrils have me convinced
it's love. Maybe that's why my heart

beat faster outside the artsy café that day,
maybe that's why I'm under the dripping canopy,
looking for the toxins, the pheromones, the evil plans.

Belabor

The end-of-summer heat brings out the animals
right on schedule, just like seventeen-year-old
cicadas. Cycle through the same tired streets

waiting for time to choose an election winner
and some wind to sweep the pretenders off the
signposts. In the countryside, tomorrow, inland

lakes leftover from glacier crawls will dapple under
the rain of flies. The necks will crane, the little fishes
winnow in. Dusk will fall. I'll be on the rented bed,

arching. Two minutes of you, a day before you start
law school in that other city. Snap. A clone in the
mirror. Six ducks flit silent across the surface.

The Lip Of

i
We'll always
have thirst faves.
We'll always have Parc's
Dollarama, the way the light
bled onto us, how you
chased after me,
the hand

I cradled the
back of your head with,
the phrase "in a perfect world,"
speaking in tongues, and the bathroom
coke that was in your blood. We'll
always have Facebook messages,
angel emojis, read receipts.
It's the little things.

ii
The street blushes
a pile of leaves. It's dark
and it is raining. The curb wet,
feet balancing at the lip of the side
walk. This is my life now,
God.

iii
I spent the whole fall
trying to catch other girls'
eyes, fresh sourdough loaf
under my arm, the black
jacket, so jaunty,

every trip a shopping trip.
Wendwork, winding, get to
know the neighbourhood,
a drill bit through dark
alleyways.

iv
Where does my money
keep going? Have you seen
the way shavings move, a shaking
saw, a chattering hum. They
collect in the cracks.

v
I bought a shirt for you.
This season's theme is black,
gold, yellow, orange, and hands
at the lip of a desk, typing
things, all those texts,

messages we should
and should not be parsing,
the push and pull of notifications,
like a dog in a park, circling, sniffing.
And at the end, you've carved
something out of nothing.
It's called subtractive
sculpture.

vi
What else is fall?
Pies—pumpkin, say,
and cherry—are not a
spectrum, dialectic, binary,
but can be kneaded 'til they feel
like one. Are you an ex
person or a why
person, etc.

vii
Coffee makes things jittery.
Our fingers hover over boards,
keys move up and down like teeth.
We still talk in code.

("cool, hi,"
"yo, sick lambo,"
"blush normative,"
"fuck you, dork,"
"post flirt.")

Now I'm spilling my
chai, jostling over the rim,
shaking hands at the
lip of the desk.

viii
Should I wear a suit jacket or
should I admit that I will never be
anything, not a writer, I'm biting
at the cusp of—

something. Can I come
clean? I can't stop thinking
about the way your mouth looks in
the story of you at the tea place. The part
in your lips. How do you take it?
Cream? Sugar?

ix
I'm losing you to law school, neuroses,
the cool friends, the cool pills, the late nights,
the coke, molly, and special K days, Instagram
likes, your boyfriend's coming back off tour,
words like "exclusive," "inappropriate,"
"shameless," "buddy," it was nice
while it lasted.

Garden Variety

Convince me to bite down. Come,
whisper up my ear a foreign
tongue. But the fruit is

astringent. Leaves an acrid taste
in the mouth, a death on the
tongue. I choke, just like

cherries. Desiccating. Then bat bad
ideas back and forth. Like dual
tongues fencing, parrying.

Jumping black widow, maybe, or else
a witch. A stray cat's eyes and the
tongue of a hapless little newt.

So kick me to the curb, blood orange;
we only ever kissed on sidewalks
anyway. Lots of plants are

poisonous but all my hidden spider
monkey veins must prefer them
anyway—the phytotoxins

bolster my resolve. Vultures haunt;
strengthening unnatural selection.
Anyway, the stinging sticks

around longer. Scorpions scuttle.
The convulsions can have me
any way they desire.

The Left-Hand Path

The north sidewalk's bathed in light;
the sun is splitting the street in two,

thinks the dual-hearted man. One
melts while the other stays frozen.

I'm of four minds about this; like my favourite
poem, Infinite Ways of Looking at a Blackbird.

I can't even go to the grocery store without
suffering from doublethink, forked tongue,

two-facedness, I Can't Believe It's Not
Dopplegängers. And the south sidewalk?

Glazed with shadow. I'm thinking about
two messages to send you, two reactions

from two yous, paper-tiger inside jokes and
paroxysms of sadness, typing in Snapchat,

two ways of laughing at a dumb
joke and two ways of being silent.

Noahtic

No snowflake
feels responsible for the avalanche and
no snap of a hunter's trap feels responsible for
the mass graves, the carcasses rotting,
the carrion dawn.

The waves will lap.
The bees will dance and whisper in our ears.
Providing counsel for a damned world. The icebergs
will calve in the heat. Ten thousand years in
the blink of an eye.

A mammoth shift.
Some things grow quick and others grow
slow. There's an arc to it: It starts off bad, gets worse,
and then ends up fine. There's a certain
je ne sais quoi to it.

It's nobody's fault,
they'll say, tears evaporating from their
ruddy faces. It's nobody's fault. Rubicund, glistening.
Yet here we wait, vestigial tails in hand,
for death's imprimatur.

So there must be
a fault, somewhere. Maybe it was our
ancestors, they'll say. Maybe the crack was baked into
the design all along. Some things grow slow
and some grow quick.

The animals will not
be loud as we kill them off. The
leaves will not be loud as they detach, slow, languid
bodies, from the evaporating trees. Until
It's all plain as day.

The icebergs will not
be loud as they calve, sacrificed
to a giant, swirling maelstrom of light and heat.
The buildings we erected will not be
loud as they crumble.

The seas will not be
loud as they step to our shorelines,
testing our hearts for weak spots. The extrapolating
tendrils of smoke will not be loud as
they encircle us one last time.

The deserts will not be loud as they smile.

Acknowledgements

Special thanks go to Ashley Opheim and Jay Ritchie for publishing this book, and to Guillaume Morissette for his thoughtful edits.

Versions of some of these poems were previously published by *The Void*, *XO Affectionate*, *Everyday Genius*, *Electric Cereal* and *Powder Keg*. Thanks to the editors of those publications.

Love and gratefulness to my incredible friends and inspirations: Shuang Liu, Brian Hastie, Emma Healey, Sruti Islam, Stephanie Barszcz, Aeron MacHattie, Domenica Martinello, Katherine Messina, Sara McCulloch, Rebecca Ugolini and Julia Wolfe.

Thank you to Arielle, my beb, for your love and support.

And none of this would have been possible without my family: Diana Halfpenny, Nathalie Manley and Frank Manley.

Alex Manley has lived in Montreal his entire life. He holds a creative writing degree from Concordia University, where he was the recipient of the 2012 Irving Layton Award for Fiction. He is left-handed.

Printed by Imprimerie Gauvin
Gatineau, Québec